D1555458

Edwin Brock was born in London in 1927. He went to local primary and grammar schools, and then served in the Royal Navy, 1945–47. He was a police constable in the Metropolitan Police in London, 1951–59, during which time he began to publish his poems. From 1959 until 1988 he was employed by a number of advertising agencies, including Mather and Crowther, J. Walter Thompson, S. H. Benson (of which he became creative group head) and Ogilvy Benson and Mather. He retired from advertising in 1988.

He published his first book, *An Attempt at Exorcism*, in 1959 (Scorpion Press). There followed a number of books, including *With Love from Judas* (Scorpion Press, 1963), a selection in the Penguin Modern Poets series, along with Geoffrey Hill and Stevie Smith (1966), *A Cold Day at the Zoo* (Rapp and Whiting, 1970), a selected poems from New Directions, New York (1972), *The Portraits and the Poses* (Secker and Warburg, and New Directions, 1973), *The Blocked Heart* (Secker and Warburg, and New Directions, 1976), *Song of the Battery Hen: Selected Poems 1959-1975* (Secker and Warburg, 1977), *The River and the Train* (Secker and Warburg, and New Directions, 1979), and *Five Ways to Kill a Man: New and Selected Poems* (Enitharmon Press, 1990). He also published a novel, *The Little White God* (Hutchinson, 1962), which was adapted as a television play and transmitted in 1964. His autobiographical book, *Here. Now. Always.*, a mixture of prose and verse, was published by Secker and Warburg, and New Directions, in 1977.

His first marriage in 1959 ended in divorce in 1964. There were two children. He married Elizabeth (Liz) in 1964, and they had one daughter, Sally ('Fred'). From the early 1970s they lived in Norfolk, where he died in September 1997.

Apart from his own poems, he was the very active poetry editor of *Ambit* from 1960 until his death. He was also a gifted potter, painter, and cultivator of *bonsai*.

EDWIN BROCK

And Another Thing

Poems 1991–1997

PREFACE BY ANTHONY THWAITE

London
ENITHARMON PRESS
1999

First published in 1999
by the Enitharmon Press
36 St George's Avenue
London N7 0HD

Distributed in Europe
by Littlehampton Book Services
through Signature Book Representation
2 Little Peter Street
Manchester M15 4PS

Distributed in the USA and Canada
by Dufour Editions Inc.
PO Box 7, Chester Springs
PA 19425, USA

ISBN 1 900564 36 X

British Library Cataloguing-in-Publication Data.
A catalogue record for this book is available
from the British Library.

Set in 10.5pt Bembo by Bryan Williamson, Frome,
and printed in Great Britain by
The Cromwell Press, Wiltshire

Preface

At the time of his death in September 1997, Edwin Brock was going through a prolific phase of writing poems. This was a late development which he found almost bewildering. After the publication of his new and selected poems, *Five Ways to Kill a Man* (Enitharmon Press), in 1990, which drew on nine collections, beginning in 1959, and which included over thirty more recent uncollected pieces, Edwin found it difficult to write. Then, in 1993, he suffered a stroke, for several weeks losing his memory and most of his ability to speak. But he made a remarkable recovery, and began to delve into the experience of the stroke and its aftermath. Many poems resulted, and these continued after cancer of the pancreas was diagnosed in the summer of 1997. He went on writing until the very end.

A few of these poems appeared here and there in the last year of his life: a dozen others have been published in various journals since his death. Edwin had preserved in five files sixty-four typescript poems written after the 1990 volume. When Liz Brock lent me the files, accompanying them was a list, in Edwin's handwriting, of all these poems, beginning with 'On the first stroke' and ending with 'Ringed by the flat horizon'. It is not clear whether this list is simply a chronological one, showing the order in which the poems were written, or whether it is a preferred running-order for some eventual book. Anyway, I have (with Liz's agreement) taken this list as my model: the forty-three poems in the present book follow its order. Some of the excluded poems seem to be late drafts rather than final versions, and indeed on some of them Edwin had written 'revise'.

ANTHONY THWAITE

Acknowledgements

Several of these poems first appeared in the following: *Ambit*, the *Guardian*, the *Independent*, the *London Magazine*, *New Writing 6* (Vintage/British Council), *Poetry Review*, *The Rialto*, and the *Times Literary Supplement*.

Contents

★

On the first stroke

Someone had murdered someone
somewhere again. It was a black space
running away from fear
and I did not know how much to give it.

It was not dying but death
of love. And not one love
but everything. It was like trying
to go straight through
from one fear to another
without love.
It was abandonment.

Someone was singing Do not forsake me
O my darling. It is for later.
When I remember. When the wind
that blows me from the beginning dies down.

It is always becoming dark
and I am worried that the ladies
allow me to walk from one night to another
with no-one to look after me.
I am afraid and pull the black blanket up
to just below my eyes and look over it.

There is a cliff road from Cromer
that flows between sand and shingle
and the cold North Sea
carrying us in black spaces of fear
above hotels and hospitals
piers and sharp white lights.

I am remembering:
It is the same voice singing
Do not forsake me O my darling
and the crying has begun.

Outside the Kings Arms Hotel on Blakeney Marshes
on the second of November in 1993
we listened to the guns and the ducks falling
from soft fantasies of sleep
and ate the crisp fish
pulled from the cold sea
and thanked the misty evening
and began again.

Convalescing in Cromer

You can come this close
to unhappiness and have the landscape
accommodate it: these small fishing boats
shudder towards Russia

but will never arrive. Always the fish
are swimming against them,
dreading the wind and the sunshine.
Almost anywhere will do this.

Remember the way our journeys
wore us into children
and then our children gave us hope . . .
Don't stay there, the beds are full of it.

This is where the sea wears out
the land and the land endures it.
Ignore the lying light years of space.
Go where you are going, warily. And report back.

Nineties Pastoral

We have been here before: Six sheep
one man and a dog. Low cloud and no rain.
Down! Up! One whistle, two whistles. Stay!
We are TV knowledgeable: know where
points are dropped and marks are gained.

Almost real, the sheep decorate
the grounds of a redundant water mill
where no flour falls, no wheel
turns and no miller sings
but like some incorrigible investment
the lawns are laundered and the roses named.

The usual dry wind. Weekend painters
make watercolours of tamed waterways.
Worms turn, and the moles avoid their traps.
On Monday mornings, the country poets
catch the London train. And
an elderly Soho roué turns to God.

The sheep stare. This is where
tin-fed cats piss in the flower beds
and holes appear in the sky.
Where somewhere along an old line
Adlestrop Station is no longer viable
and the birds have gone.

Thank heavens . . .

Especially when this soft wind comes up
from the South on its lung-kissing scent
of rotting wrack, it brings back
those things I'd rather forget

as, pampered by age and wasted breath,
I sit out this summer's drought
under a low East Anglian sky
that, heavy with rain, hoards it
for a few small Cromer crabs
and the remains of that one childhood day
I keep to prophesy the weather.

Alive in this last limbo, I was glad
when they said unto me
let us go into the garden and look for
that moment when the seaweed drops,
sweat dries and we are within
a day's distance of being better

and, remembering each and every one of those
whose beginnings I knew and then blighted,
wonder whether it is too late
to ask forgiveness and preposterous
to look for love – yet they are given,
which makes heaven a less distant prospect
and death an altogether cosier convention.

October at Burnham Overy Staithe

'Owdoo . . . fair day . . . sharp frost tonight!'
he pedals past on the rutted coastal footpath
his heavy back making straight for the North Sea
leaving me wondering whether his frost prophecy
will come true. Owdoo!

It is called passing–the–time–of–day
and I have never known why the day needs
to be passed nor whether, long before watches
and weather forecasts, these seers, these
perambulating seaweeds, covered England
passing its time. Fair day you
reefer–jacketed ghost, you antique of English heritage!

Nelson was born near here
and his wig–framed face decorates
every village pub sign. Owdoo!
Did you too smell out fair weather
and pass its time around the fleet?

It is now; the lowest of low tides:
cabin cruisers capsize upon the ribbed land
and sailing boats in winter wrapping
rattle their chains. Dried grasses
pick up the wind and pass it on
to the salt marshes and samphire.
Fair day . . . fare well . . . and bon voyage!
it is good to be here in autumn sunshine
knowing I will be gone before
tonight's sharp frost kills the red geraniums
and cracks the pots in my comfortable garden.

Like father like daughter

Those two unpruned apple trees
at the end of my grandfather's garden:
black-skeletoned they produced
lemon-sour apples the size of golf balls.

That outside privy which smelt of darkness
and damp newspaper; and the barrel
of floating horse-turds which stood
under the trees in a cloud of buzzing blueflies.

My mother's monologue: of the hairdresser
who wanted to kiss her, and the shopkeeper
who told her: *the trouble with you is
you've got champagne taste and four-ale bar money.*

She wore these compliments, as she saw them,
like a tinsel halo which shimmered
through all her days, like sunlight
catching the wings of her father's buzzing blueflies.

Arrangement in grey and black

Whistler's mother was probably not
that dominating triangle
watching from the edge of darkness

but some frail old lady
living out her last years
on supplementary benefits
in sheltered accommodation

visited by the home help,
a caring neighbour or,
on high days, her GP.

And her son? He's there
on the other side of darkness
trying to sort out night from
nightmare, faith from fear
and dying for something happy to happen.

The first song

We went to buy trout
to stock his two lakes
to be fished for by the hour
by businessmen to take
home with their manhoods slaked.

The water boiled with them
at the pellets the kids threw to them
bought by the pound from a shop selling
the privilege of feeding their trout.

We went to buy a trout
with a Worcestershire farmer
forsaking his soil for a new drama
of quiet fish hiding
in the shadows of his deepest stones.

And later sat by the lakes
in the middle of orchards
that grew as many temptations
as any other Eden:

especially when the blossom blew
head-high around us
like new snow drifting
across an old plain.

Then, biting the fruit in the mellow days,
we knew the hot summers,
our fingers in cool water and the fish
in the shadows of their stones.

But as the days shortened
in the small towns between villages
and the married women dragged adulteries
before the listening magistrates

a strange fish
still wet from its own shadow
rose from beneath a stone
to slide like something entirely new
between the gnarled roots
of the older trees.

Fuckaduck!

The season began in early summer:
thirteen of them whistled behind their white mother
as we ran to the baker for dry bread
saying How will she rear so many?
and These will be fed by faith hope and charity!

On the following day we thought we had miscounted:
six could not be missing presumed so quickly dead.
And are mother ducks so mathematically stupid
they cannot calculate the sum of minus half a brood?

By the third day we were waking pale into nightmare
saying with our first breath Good morning!
How many are there left? Still she marched on
looking resolutely ahead and keeping tight
to a route which traversed minefields
of cats and moorhens, killer fish and motor cars
leaving behind a debris of dying expectations.

Now it is this humid July afternoon.
Curtained by willows and willow herb
and lulled by the background music
of an idyllic mill race, I hear
the last yellow duckling's tiny whistle
choke in the throat of our legendary pike.

No flower stops growing,
the mother duck is unperturbed
and I do not know whether my curse is calling
to fish or water, duck, Darwin or God.

Those were the days

In October
they drained the public swimming pool
of its chlorinated water
and covered the booming space
with flush-fitting floorboards
waxed to carry the shuffling weight
of girls in fading suntans.

In October
across the beat of the Ted Heath band
and the long notes of its Canadian crooner
they sang the Saturday nights
into Old Buttermilk Skies and Perdido
and Brylcreemed boys in utility suits
danced myths into their histories.

In November's smog
the dancehalls lit a beacon
above the bombed-out terraces
short rations and bleak nagging mothers
and all the saxophones were dreaming
of a white Christmas still to come.

Balloons and spotlights
baubles and beer celebrated Christ's birth
and at midnight the Christmas crowd
spilled over into candlelit churches:
it was a time of singing and of paradox.

Until January
when the dances died down
like summer flowers and the sounds
of chlorinated water and screams began
and someone in the street outside
was singing the same songs over and over
like a fly in amber
like someone who has married the wrong wife.

In amber

All the way down from the camp
was a slippery cliff path
with a small hut that sold ices

then the wide white sand
to the sea and the sky all together

later, tar bubbles boiled in the roads
and the blue sky
was smeared with the brush marks
of tiny aeroplanes.

By winter the trees in Dulwich Park
had dressed themselves
and the golf course was like Switzerland

it was a village of Christmases
looking backwards and forward

as though someone I loved
had died
and I had not noticed.

Retreat

We tried to sit beside this pool
inside the sound of water
and see forever nothing but green

as though some kind of coverlet
of meadow sweet and willow herb
birdsong and blossom were sewn

into forgetfulness. But had forgotten
the mouse in an owl's claw
night in a child's eyes

and the way a pheasant cries as though
its throat is torn and its wings
are driving its ghost away.

Morston Marshes

Into this muddy coastline
the North Sea seeps silently
twice a day
under the kestrel's weather eye

in the growing puddles
gulls drill the marsh
for nothing we can see
or screech their territory
like fishwives
from the tops of poles

even in August
the sky drowns us
in small drops
settling on hair and eyes
wanting us flying in it
or grovelling in the ooze
at the water's edge

I died in this country
and came back
to pay my debt
to its wetlands

something fishes me
all the way
back to where it began

and is beginning again
down the years
with a million denials.

The ghost dancer

It is surprising to be here, now,
among these people at the end.
Far away, or so it seems, from
anywhere where anything happened.
The tiny river Tas drags its heels
past our windows, barely able
to push aside the willowherb and reeds.
The swans have flown to deeper water
and one pike has cleared the pond.

Yet it has happened to someone,
as surely as the ghost we saw
that wild autumn evening
dancing downhill beside
my father's grave. It was more real
than any question of belief,
more substantial.
I can still feel the wind in the trees
and the unaccountable silence
waving us away.

None of us wants less than this:
looking over the strands
of history
to one moment of memory
recalled in love.

Cromer

Let's not talk about the past
too many people have taken
too many parts of it
and are always running
just short of the horizon.

Postcards arrive from
practically anywhere they are;
some of them still living
and still running;
usually shiny photographs
of impossibly blue water.

Let's not talk about today
while we are still busy in it
looking at small things
which run across the roads
to disappear forever.

Just yesterday
is near enough behind to feel.
But over, blissfully over.

Like the day we discovered
Cromer
coming across it, apparently
like a gap
on the left of the world,
bright with the palest of light
milky as though angels
could fly in it
or sit fishing
at the end of the pier
and we could go down
all those cliff steps
and join them
for just the rest of the day.

After which we came back
over and over again
and it was never the same
but adjusted itself
to small growing girls
and a young Mongol
who cried 'faster and faster!'
exploding cake crumbs
from her mouth
like a snowstorm
in bright sunshine.

Or days in October
when the blizzard wind
blew the hospital nightmares
from my eyes
in huge tears
which split into
a million rainbows.

Let's just talk about that
and let it not come
any nearer than this moment
when we are trying
to tie love all around it
and decide
who to invite in
for the rest of our memory.

Villainelle

Ma Thatcher was the catcher in the Rye
At least she caught us all once she'd begun
By market forces we must live or die

After the laughter came the need to cry
Too late, by then the damage had been done
Ma Thatcher was the Catcher in the Rye

You must have heard the costermonger's cry
'Now would I try to catch you Honeybun!'
And how the market forces him to lie

Shareholders say the limit is the sky
Where heaven waits for those who fought and won
Or so Ma Thatcher sang from in the Rye

Of course it is much easier to buy
Room at the top if you're the topdog's son
By market forces you will live, not die

But we know when Icarus tried to fly
And came unstuck up by the midday sun
Ma Thatcher couldn't catch him in the Rye
By mythic forces he must live and die.

Moules marinières

Charlie Webb told us where to find them
and the time of low tide
so we went there, four of us,
each with an old knife and a supermarket bag.

We found the bay on King Arthur's doorstep
scrubbed white by the punctual Atlantic
and gleaming in the low sunlight.
We blamed the bruises our feet made
and tiptoed from rock to rock whispering
each new discovery: the most decorous
beachcombers in musseling's long history.

Until we found the cave: frightening us
with the weight above its black
hollow. But we went in.
And robbed it. It was like that morning
in Barnes' field with the warm rain
falling and the mushrooms springing
in rings from his cow-cropped grass
and ourselves knowing we had too many
but unable to stop for giggling
and hugging each other.

It was like that, but different:
all night we left them spinning
in clean water to stuff themselves silly
on Sainsbury's oatmeal. Then
we boiled them in onion, garlic and wine
and ate until the whole Cornish coastline
flowed in us and banged us like Drake's drum.

Postcard from Wells-next-the-Sea

I am up here to get away
from everything. I have told
the neighbours the river is rising
but they have palmed me off
with some talk about getting
an expert in. Besides which
I think they believe I am eccentric
and see problems where none exist.

So I came up here to this midwinter
hotel-break right on the bum
of Britain and thought: The bloody
North Sea won't give me any rising
damp problems, which was wrong
because I'm always reading reports about
crumbling coastlines and global warming
and how the whole lot's going to be awash
in next to no time. But that's
on another time-scale, by which
my grandson will have spent
my money and forgotten me.

In the meantime, the Crown Hotel
still sells a choice of three real ales
in its cosy bar, and the full breakfast
will get you through most of the day.
Time to watch the boats subside
as the sea is sucked out of the estuary
and climb creaking to their feet again
as it all comes hurrying back.
Time to walk to those skeletal pines
behind the stilted bathing shacks
and believe the whole world is fossilised.

Which means of course you cannot bear
to think of it going on without you there:
'Once and no more' as Rilke once said
and found it some kind of comfort.

And there is still time to wish
you had been born here and grown up
doing the kind of things these people
seem to do: a pottering around lobster
pots, and a cracking around crabs
in a snowstorm of shrieking gulls.

I came here to get away from
the rising river, but even so
my feet are wet. I believe if I
stand here much longer the pond
will creep up to my neck, getting
blacker and muddier as the hours pass.
There are even gulls this far in
from the surrounding sea; and crab shells
everywhere. It is cold. I have told
the neighbours, and an expert is on his way.

Winterton

It is a sinking
into sand; marram grass
too sharp to lie on; eyes
stinging in the wind, and
a nerve in the cheek jumping
like an actor playing Dostoevsky.

A few memories remain:
the seal pup
dragging its wound up the beach
showing a ripped belly
and crying for help;
terns dive-bombing
the air above their nests;
the flotsam fox
bitten and chewed
scourged and scraped
but still recognisable

and always the grey North Sea
disappearing into a grey sky.

Beachcombing between the season's
limbs to discover
loneliness

or coming off the frost-crisp dunes
rejoicing in ownership.

Sixty-eight years should burst
the walls of a skull with this;
but mostly it drifts
like fine sand, or bangs
against the groynes whenever
the wind blows towards the land.

Obit

Imagine a love being broken
on the fourth floor of a Council flat!
A window is left open.
The words upon the welcome mat
are wiped away. The night
comes in to stay, and the phone is silent.

Something like a dog leaving home
makes its way downhill
beneath the silver streetlamps.
Like early pictures of the moon.
Like children woken too soon.
Like all the words that will be spoken
still unsaid, or dreamed upon.

The calendar is on the wall
but no-one has thought
to mark it. No-one believes
that anything has happened. No-one
saw the dog go, phoned a friend
or waited for the world to arrive.

Somebody should have shut out
the night air. Lit a candle in the window.
Stared out all the dark imaginings.
And seen what the dawn was bringing
with wide-awake eyes.

Snow

I have as many ways
of saying I am sorry
as an Eskimo has
of explaining snow

often the windows
seem to leave
the sunlight out of sight,
its red glow
like a ghost
that has passed without
looking in

it is an experience
which speaks only
from hollow to hollow:
a room
where someone has been
or may arrive

where I could learn to sit
cross-legged with sorrow
as a mantra:
an anticipation
of love
that time and only time
may describe.

Keeping mum

In those days the streets
might have hidden anything:
my mother's lover in an old car
in an accident. Don't tell her!

We were in winter uniforms
and the blue streetlights
stretched our shadows from
Heaton Arms to Peckham Rye.

We were untouchable.
Don't tell her, he said.
One eye could not look me straight;
it was pale and watering
like an animal which has bulk
without strength. And was dying.
It was a shape which shivers
between trees. Or in doorways.

I have stood here before
waiting to hear the owl cry
or the moon moving up behind me.
Only my shadow had no dreams
of women and would not die
until the morning came
and the streetlights ended.

My back as I walked away
had no pity. My heels struck
the frosted paving stones. And the shops
were like a fairground in sunlight.

Alma Mater

I was there before the blacks
moved up from Brixton
to push the Irish hordes away

When there was barely room
on Saturdays to squeeze
between the fug-filled pubs

When the trams clanged bells
and struck electric sparks
from trolley poles

And the coppers patrolled
in twos or sat quietly
in their station-clubs.

I feel her there now
shrunken in her Council room,
a history reduced to dust

And I feel her hand
fidgeting as it holds mine.
Never still and never silent.

The first fist I had to overcome,
the one I learned to dodge
and run away.

I still try to pray for light
between us, singing
canticles of filial love

Until our Christmas cards cross
bringing
wishes Twelfth Night will remove.

The hopscotch game

Someone will have a stick of chalk
and there's no problem about
the drawing – a sort of folk Mondrian
without the colour. The numbers
one to eight, four on either side,
and the box at the top marked OXO.

It is all the children need to know:
the stone thrown to the right square
and hopping there and back again. They have
at least this claim on everything we do.

Called indoors before the storm breaks,
they are fractious, sulk in their early beds,
strain their ears to the words bled
from all the rooms around them
or, worse, wait for silence
as doors slam and they interpret
footsteps as absences.

It will always be like this.
At the end of journeys someone
will be sending postcards back
of views of blue skies and white cliffs.
They will be asked for love
and learn the language of collusion.

Here in the city streets again
they chalk upon the paving stones,
and sometimes OXO at the end of a game
is replaced by the word HOME.

Both ends

I saw my son born
in the bed-sitting room
of a first-floor flat
in grimy Camberwell Green
after talking to the midwife
about Freud.

I saw my first corpse
on a mortuary slab
opened for a post-mortem
with a class of policemen
after talking to the inspector
about the dead.

I still know them both:
the now middle-aged friend
and the then middle-aged stranger,
still think of them from time to time;
knowing that the time for one
runs into its own future
and the time for the other
runs into mine.

Piscatory jingle

The trouble was
it was unthinkable

think of the worst
that can happen
and it will

the trouble with poison is
it's not undrinkable

you enjoy it
savour it
until you're full

the trouble is
the sun will burn you

melt your wings
and throw you down

and rain will rain you
drench you
drain you
wash you in it
until you drown

don't ask
for anything
don't wish
one wish

let every
sleeping dog
lie still

then you may
walk upon
the water

or would you
rather be
a fish?

February 6 a.m.

Displaced by dreaming
the whole world seems down
and dawn comes
in a cold sulk

no more than a memory
of other mornings
when air and water
were their own light

by the side of the pond
that alder
is waiting for its tree-creeper
which has
deserted it today

something is shining
the edges
of the cloud curtain
and shaping
the horizon
of crowded trees

three small birds
peck the hard ground
and guard their territory

it is a beginning

A special offering

Soon as we hear the churchbells
on a Sunday morning now we're off
to visit Waitrose, wouldn't miss it anyhow

the quiet numinousity of automatic doors
the shining aisles where gleaming angels tread
the pre-wrapped little fishes and the Unblessed bread

the Bulgarian 95 red altar wine
that's never known the arteries of Christ
but counts its blessings still at 2.99

and every day's a harvest festival
whose autumn splendour falls
upon the West wall's Warhol cans

to duplicate the ornament
of stained glass in Chartres
or candle-power in Notre Dame

only this morning a dear old soul
stroked himself dead beside
an amazing grace of cut-price lamb

there was something Biblical about it
as though the bells had summoned us
to witness man's humanity to man.

On the road

'Sure you don't want to worry about
little tings like dat!' you said.

We were halfway around Ireland
with you driving from Dublin to Cork

before you told me you didn't have
a driving licence and had never passed a test.

'Sure you don't want to worry about
little tings like dat!' So I didn't.

We were looking for the goodness of Guinness
to drink it all over the South

or as much of it as we could manage
to praise the goodness of its maker.

So we drank it down to soothe
our consciences between the Irish coffee

breakfasts, the gin and tonic lunches
and the wine and brandy dinners.

★

'Look at those bastards!' you'd say
in every hotel dining room, pointing out

the priests, their dog-collars softened
by discreet lighting and their faces warmed

by the glow from their balloon glasses.
'Bastards!' you'd say as we lived it up

from Killarney's lakes to Galway Bay
on the fat of the land and our Guinness a day

singing the songs of the IRA
to twanging strings and a tin whistle.

★

In that October every tourist trap was sprung
and low cloud rested on the green fields
and grey dry-stone walls. We were drunk

in the backs of barber shops and greengrocers
or sometimes in the parlours of isolated cottages,
joining in the one conversation which murmured

its low masculine note into the darkness,
or waited in the Holy Hour for the black stout
to slow to a dribble of poetry.

'Sure you don't want to worry about
tings like dat!' you said
as we watched Nelson's statue explode

at the top of O'Connell Street,
and you gave me a piece of its speckled granite
to use as a souvenir paperweight.

★

It was a good fortnight we had illegally on the road
in the days of the Behans and Edna O'Brien

when it was easy to whoop the rebel cry
and romanticise the freedom fighters

as, wearing the green and waving
a flaming sword, you stepped out

43

of your London urbanity into a fantasy
of young men whispering on dark corners.

★

Back in London the rain had lost its softness
and was cold. The fields that were planted

between the rows of traffic were dying of people,
and winter was on sale in the lighted shops.

We sat in the peace of a panelled pub
drinking foreign lager and planning the fights

we would watch at Wembley, making a life
out of almost nothing as conscientiously

as we'd once drunk Guinness among resented priests
and sung the songs of its murdering heroes.

Charlie Wood's summer

His voice ran around that summer
like pegtops and scooters: 'Charlie's here!
Here comes Charlie!'
and his sunstruck head beaconed
above the Eldorado ice-cream trike
as he called us to the school gates:
'I'm Charlie Wood . . . and I've got
a little bit of good! You never
wanna miss Charlie!'

'Bloody Charlie Wood . . . !'
my mother said.

That summer was the first,
and we never saw him after it:
he came out of Goodrich Road
and never returned there.
But while he was with us
we eased each other aside
to become his audience.
He told us he'd trained
to be a doctor, and we believed him.
He told us we wore our belts
too tight, pushing his fingers
into our waistbands,
and we loosened them.

'Bloody Charlie Wood . . . !
Bloody doctor!' my mother said.

He left his stories hanging
on the late bell, and rang them again
when school came out.
He told us about the boy,
about our age, who'd fallen
from a swing and ruptured himself,

and how, to silence the screams,
he'd punched him on the point of the jaw
'Not hard enough to hurt him,
but just enough to make him unconscious'
and then manipulated the displaced testicle,
making hospitals and ambulances unnecessary.

I didn't tell my mother.
'Bloody Charlie Wood!
Bloody rupture!' she'd have said.

We didn't hear his voice again,
but all through autumn we chorused
'Charlie's 'ere!' and practised
punching each other on the point of the jaw
just hard enough to cause unconsciousness.
Nobody I knew
ever stood still long enough
to find out if it were true.

But 'Bloody Charlie Wood . . . !'
my mother said. 'Where's he now?'

Goodbye

There was no need for you to die,
you could easily have found a place
outside Tesco's store where
the ring-pierced share
their rubbish with mongrel dogs
and the city blows its history
around bare feet.

There, squeezed between the bodies
of a reluctant audience, you
could repeat your story:
'We didn't go looking for trouble
but if anyone wanted it . . . !'
that litany you learned
at your father's knee.

The street words vary, but the message
is the same: Absent fathers
dumb mothers, and all the love
drowned in that white spirit
you could always, somehow, obtain.

Down the road, inside the cathedral,
they say there is the memory
of a man who knew you
and wanted your company,
but he is buried now
under centuries of East Anglian stone
and the voices of his admirers,
none of whom could have known
you or where you came from.

A boyhood five times over
was enough! Scarcely time
to get you out of knee-length shorts
and away from Camberwell dust,
but time enough to make a family
which hates each moment of your memory.

Now, underground or burned,
whatever they decide to do with you,
there's no holding back:
You were a drunk, and not
a pleasant one at that! No, not a drunk,
for that has a matey tone!
You were a lonely alcoholic
and, God help us, you died alone.

Can we sentimentalise what's left
and assume you acquired the good sense
dying brings? If so, you'll know
the emptiness which drove you to drink
still lives in us. Cheers brother!
Knock it back and choke on this: it is
not over until the fat lady sings.

These old songs . . .

grow in the mind,
their rhymes chiming endlessly
with the sound of feet walking
or rain falling or being taken up
by garden birds, one line at a time.

Landmarks, favourite stones,
reminders of moments
that only history makes important,
we hum them down to immortality

so that now they fence us in
with the faces of lost opportunities,
and all the moons and Junes that ever were
are meadow-larking above England.

For her birthday
on June 13 1996

This poem about you
will be in a book
called Poems About You

and on the cover
will be one of those
luminous paintings

Bonnard made of his wife
in the bath where her breasts
and the water are

the same temperature
and it is impossible to tell
by touch where one

becomes the other and
the light from the window
mixes them into one

it is saying you are
this reality and I cannot know
where you end and the rest

begins but it is not the poem
I want to write about you
which would make my flesh rise

as at the beginning
and carry me crying
back towards birth.

And another thing . . .

Why in Christ's name
can't somebody say something?
Nothing profound, just:
It's OK under ground
the dirt doesn't get into your eyes!
Or: *you'd be surprised*
at the sounds that come down,
breezes, birdsong and heavy breathing!
I mean, who needs
that Yorick sentimentality?
We want the bloody *skull* speaking!

And what about those friends
who've been through the fire?
Just a whisper as the smoke
flies higher to say: *it's OK*
you never feel the blisters!
An everyday postcard will do,
nothing as festive as Easter!
You see, it isn't our mortality
we fear, that's neither here
nor anywhere; it's the thought
of all that emptiness up there
that takes your breath away.

Thy will be done

People are dying all around her:
a son, a son-in-law, what few
friends are still trying to keep up.

Every time a door opens you wonder
who will leave, as though a room
is emptying itself to make space.

She knows the road to the crematorium
as well as the shops she knew
in the days when she could get around.

Knows the holy words the vicar
or priest or preacher intones, even though
they have less meaning than a lawyer's prose.

Sits now through her days without fear;
is not really here at all, except for
a few small commonplace pains.

Cannot remember her happiest time,
when she was seventeen, in a foxtrot
which might easily have been a waltz.

After the headlines

It is easier now:
a turning autumn tide
slaps the beach at Cromer
combing its fingers back
through rattling shingle;
the crab boats ride
the low sunshine, each
towards its own rusty tractor,
each named after
the crew's two wives,
Valerie and Teresa, Christine and Vi;
the last of the season's visitors
line the pier's white rails
to watch them in, and
under the wind the North Sea
shifts its cunning counterpane
uncovering small children and suicides.

Every summer ends as suddenly
as before, yet still surprises.
It is a time for counting and accountability.
In the pub that overlooks the bay
a lifeboat man describes
how the two children looked
after a week washed by the sea.
Not only wind wets our eyes.
We dry them, drink and try
not to disturb the suicides.

Walking with neighbours
(for A and A)

On a Sunday a single sad bell
would lie across this autumn soil
like its own funeral procession;
but a grey Saturday
waiting for tomorrow
can give an impression of reality:
religion is not a necessity.

For instance, the flints still call
from the walls of older barns
and even the roof reeds show impatience;
small roads are worn upon the neighbourhood
like black armbands, and the silence
cannot hold its tongue in this mood.

All birthday cards are elegiac now:
the names of everyone we've known
clutter the verges, or are blown
across the empty fields of a dry season.
And following our footsteps
through gaps in their hawthorn hedge
overweight white turkeys huddle together and holler
like the condemned calling to the newly-dead.

Visiting Brent Eleigh

Christ has been over this country,
His sand-hot feet on its wet soil.
He has broken through the walls
of its mediaeval churches
to drag Adam burning
from the round suckhole of hell.

His was the face behind a bird,
a hand torn from wood
its flesh mauled
to make the moment of love.

It was his body
hanging above
cupped and hungry hands
to understand
their loss and their loneliness.

For two thousand years
he has drawn together
this landscape of English history
which we may know and visit
and buy serially
in postcards at each door.

Sleeping pills

After the snow
the grass grows again.
What have I forgotten?

A poem can start with anything
provided it ends with poetry.

Minton said that, about painting.
And the saddest picture I have
is of him dancing in Muriel's
ignored by the afternoon drinkers.

I have lived too much for sorrow;
but last year's death
of mother, brother, oldest friend
have left hollows no time
can fill; and on these
frozen nights the draughts
attack my face and chill
my dreams.

*

After the snow
the grass grows:
when my mouth
was between her thighs
and my ear
at the base of her abdomen
the sound
was like a sung Eucharist
in a small parish church
deep down underwater.

Worrying which one of us
will go first keeps me
awake at night;
that and the cold around my eyes.

★

Here's that johnny
with the pastel shirt
and the parson's collar:
his wife is pregnant again.

What have I forgotten?
BC, AD, NOW.

After the snow
the grass grows
and is unsettling.

This box in my head
has red walls
papered with poetry:

BC, AD, NOW.
AD, BC, NOW.

Ghost story

Did she ever really say:
'You look as though you've seen a ghost'?

The omens were always there:
the black cemetery trees
at the bottom of teacups,
the daily horoscopes
and, in the dust-dry air,
a willing substitution
of astrology for faith.

Silent on storm-debris
dancing on water there
'Go away! Go!'
And fear-shaken we ran.

'You look as though you've seen a ghost!'
she said. Round-faced from a kitchen stove.
It wasn't. It was only our future
visiting us out of time.

Moyra

I knew her when her husband
drew her nude shape in charcoal
to hang on the wall beside portraits
of jazz musicians. And I have a photograph
of the two of us sitting together, naturally,
in the quiet corner of a noisy party
sheltering from too much talking.
And other moments of other parties, joining in.
I do not have photographs of the years between:
the upheavals of illness and moving house.
Nor can I imagine how we both grew into now.

I wish she had not told me what she sees
passing herself in shopwindows.
Of course she is not that person,
nor am I me. It is the streets that have changed
everything: with indifference and the way
they write themselves into every growing history.

Lost and Found

There were no bullrushes,
only dark green whorls of canadensis,
and along the water's edge
a gathering crowd of mostly women
quiet and staring, as though their eyes
could drag something to the surface
perhaps trailing bubbles of breath.

She, of course, was alone in sunshine;
maybe a breeze rattled the dry reeds
so that a baby's cry could be lost,
so that she passed by, stopped,
came back, hesitated before parting
the curtain, wondering who would believe her.

Skies change from egyptian blue to
camberwell grey, life changes:
these women are the same chorus
that cries beside collapsing mines;
rain falls in the same dark way and
the slated rooftops know everything.

Ringed by the flat horizon

Getting there wasn't good:
the car tyres on the gravel,
the villages and early-morning people.
Is this the worst moment?
I asked every moment.

The pills I had taken to stop
the images working on my brain
weren't working: over and over again
the knife made its own decisions
without even knowing my name.

Ringed by the flat horizon
we scan each moment
trying to recognise it,
and hoping we have paid
for its existence.

Moonscape. Dust. Solar wind.
Our souls are spoken through
Stephen Hawking's voice box
and are no easier to understand.

Goodness is somewhere in
the things that move us,
and those quiet thoughts
that surprise us
with their lucidity. Do not

forsake me O my darling,
you have always been where
understanding is, and able
to understand.

LIST OF SUBSCRIBERS

Dannie Abse
Anna Adams
David Annwn
Donald Arlett
Amanda and Simon Badger
Phil and Marlene Badger
Peter Baldwin
Jonathan Barker
Ruth Barker
Paul Barnes
Benjamin Bax
Martin and Judy Bax
Tim Bax
Julian Earwaker and Kathleen
    Becker
Virginia Bedini
Jon-Pier Bee
David Bell
Oliver Bernard
David Bernstein
Alan Berry
Sue Bethell
Elizabeth Bewick
Pat Blanchard
The Bleach Family
Alison Brackenbury
Malcolm Bradbury
Neville Braybrooke
Elizabeth Brock
Fred Brock
Hazel Brock
Lucy Brock
Mike Brock
Nicholas Brock
Rebecca Brock
James Brockway

Virginia Brookes
Brotherton Collection,
    University of Leeds
Alan and Sandy Brownjohn
Nadine Brummer
Romi Bryden
Jim Burns
David Burns-Garside
Alan Byford
Moyra Caldecott
Jenna Cazalet
Tom Chitty
Alan Clodd
Dominic and Marcus Cole
Peter Cole
David and Liz Coleman
Chris Cook
Doreen and Geoff Cook
Matthew Cook
Michael and Barbara Copp
John Cotton
Kevin Crossley-Holland
Martyn Crucefix
Neil Curry
David and Lorraine Dawson
Peter and Lynda English
Nick Evans
Ronald Ewart
U. A. Fanthorpe and
    R. V. Bailey
Pat Fenn
Duncan Forbes
Robin Fournel
Richard Fowler
E. G. Fox
Peggy Fox

Joy Francis
Auriel Gibson
John D. Gibson
Malcolm Gluck
Di Gold
Mark Goodwin
Alasdair Gordon
Joan Gregory
David Grubb
Douglas Haines
Frank Hall
Steven Halliwell
Jack and Jan Harrison
Margaret and David Harrop
Anne Harvey
Diana Hendry
Lorraine Hendy
Michael and Tricia Henry
Ivan and Dawne Hill
Roger Hobdell
Angela Huth
Jan Jenkins
David and Helen Johnson
Rosemary Jost
R. Keeton
Rosalind Kent
Mimi Khalvati
John Killick
Caroline and Bruce Leckie
R. T. L. Lee
Sonia Lindqvist
Edwin McCloughan
Hank and Barbara McCloughan
Lucy McCloughan
Meade McCloughan
Ian McKelvie
Michael Mackmin
Elizabeth Marais
E. A. Markham

Peter Meares
Kathryn Michael
Michael Millgate
Ken and Stella Milne
George and Sue Milner-Smith
John Mole
John Montgomery
Hubert Moore
Sarah and Peter Moore
Derek and Christina Morris
Madeline Munro
Jean Naylor
John and Elizabeth Nicholls
Peter Nicolson
Paddy Nolan
Rosemary Norman
Griselda Ohannessian
Masa Ohtake
David Page
Jeremy Page
Peter Porter
Valerie Purton
Simon Rae
D. E. R. Ransome
Alan Rodford
John and Melanie Rolph
Tom Rosenthal
Alan Ross
Frauke and Philip Ross
Patricia Ross
Jacqueline and John Rout
David and Stephanie Ryland
Carole Satyamurti
Myra Schneider
Cecilia Scurfield
Perviz Seabrook
The Seagrove Family
Virginia and Sylvan Shendler
Chris Skilton Smith

William Spencer
Enid and Chris Stephenson
Edward Storey
Stephen Stuart-Smith
George Szirtes
Len Taylor
Royston Taylor
Howard Temperley
Alice Thwaite
Ann and Anthony Thwaite
Emily Thwaite and Bill
    Sanderson
Lucy Thwaite and Matthew
    Dodd-Noble
Joy and David Tinson
Jonathan Trench
William Trevor

Michael Trollope
Edward Upward
Edward Vanderpump
Rajeev Vinaik
John Wakeman
Alan Wallwork
Peter Warren
Katherine Weaver
Charles and Eileen Webb
Patty and Peter Wightman
Janet Wilkes
Gwen Williamson
Joseph Wolf
William Wolf
Owen and Clare Wood
Constance Yates